The Unfinished Journey

The Unfinished Journey

Firdevs Dede

Published by **Xlibris** in Feb 2012

Published by **Xlibris** in Feb 2012
Copyright © Firdevs Dede 2012
Front cover image © Firdevs Dede
Book illustration © Firdevs Dede
Back cover photo © Firdevs Dede

A CIP catalogue record for this title is available from the British Library.

ISBN: Hardcover   978-1-4653-0226-7
           Softcover   978-1-4653-0225-0
           Ebook   978-1-4653-0224-3

First edition published in Feb 2012

Correspondence address with the author: firdevs.dede@gmail.com

Author's web site address: **www.firdevsdede.com**

This book was printed in the United States of America.

To order additional copies of this book, contact:
Xlibris Corporation
0-800-644-6988
www.xlibrispublishing.co.uk
Orders@xlibrispublishing.co.uk
302437

Contents

Foreword

Poetry writing fascinates me a great deal. I've been exploring poetry as a lyrical language to describe my inner reality since I was 18. There is always a close link between my poetry and my visual artwork. Many titles for my paintings and drawings come from my poems. Over the years, the semantic nature of my poetry has been developed alongside my academic interests in various subject matters. Poetry doesn't only represent my sentiment as a poet, but also reveals my interest to science. Life cannot be separated from ill health and death. Whatever a poet experiences in life can be a source of inspiration to develop further in the architectural structure of poetry writing. When a poet builds up the skeleton of a poem by placing each word in its correct place one by one like a brick, which holds the essence of the construction together without falling apart, a poet's dream is already accomplished without any compromise.

For my first poetry book entitled "**The Unfinished Journey**", I had compiled the poems with the various themes produced over 34 years' duration. In this edition, I have included my early poems such as "**The Song of Life**", "**True Love**", "**And**", "**Integrity**", "**Lullaby**", "**A Mistake Beyond Repair**" and "**Noise**" which were all written when I was in Istanbul, where I was born and had lived till the age of 20. I left Istanbul to work as an art teacher in the northern part of Anatolia in Turkey for two years between 1981 and 1983. I resigned from my civil servant occupation as a secondary school art teacher in order to pursue my artistic career in London. Since then I have been producing my visual artwork as well as writing poetry by highlighting the significance of the places I have been and the people I have met.

I have inherited my poetical sensitivity from my poet father Durmus Dede and my mother Hamdiye Dede. My parents loved animals and the beautiful nature of countryside. We had cats, dogs, rabbits, silk warms and a partridge living with us at home. I was taken to the most beautiful seaside resources to discover the wildlife. The sea had been at the heart of my life as a child. I was never far away from the sea in my birthplace in Istanbul. However, living in London makes me long for the seaside. I am inclined to go to the places by the sea when I search for a suitable theme for my photographical exploration. I expect this book will give readers a flavour of my poetry. It has been a great pleasure for me to compile the selected poems for this book. I hope to share my love of poetry with poetry readers.

Firdevs Dede
Jan 2012 London

The Song of Life

Textile Image, Pen Drawing

© Firdevs Dede 2000

THE SONG OF LIFE

Have you ever listened to the sound of life
                       attentively?

Have you ever heard the dawn-chorus' singing
                       during the spring time?

Have you ever found a delight in seagulls' screams
                       by the seaside?

Have you ever listened to the sound of the waves
                       in the stormy days?

Have you ever sung the song of life
                 despite the anger of the sea
                       and the noise of the rain?

The joy for the present time
                 is only in the song of life
                       now!

© Firdevs Dede

July 1977 Istanbul

True Love

Textile Image, Pen Drawing

© Firdevs Dede 2000

TRUE LOVE

True love is not limited
Love for the people or the places we know
                    is not adequate

Love should be expanded for the humanity
                    worldwide

Love for the flowers we've never seen before

Love for all the fish in the oceans
            without even knowing
                  their proper names
                      by heart

Love for the world's peace

Love for art

Love for integrity

Love for decency

Love for generosity

Love for the entire cosmos

Love for others

Love for ourselves

Love for life

Love for the dead

True love is an unlimited edition
                of our human hearts

© Firdevs Dede

August 1977 Istanbul

Integrity

Textile Image, Pen Drawing

© Firdevs Dede 2000

INTEGRITY

If we speak the truth
                but
                        only the truth

We need to lead a life with integrity

Needless to say
                there is no life without any error

Nonetheless
                life with fewer mistakes
                                is more valuable

© Firdevs Dede

September 1979 Istanbul

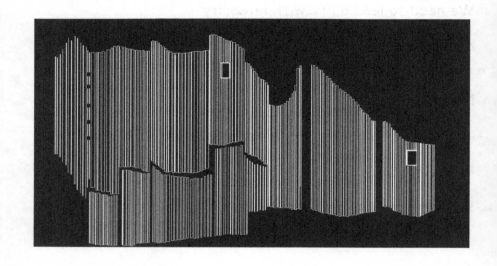

Lullaby

Digital Drawing

© Firdevs Dede 1998

LULLABY

Close your eyes
    and sleep my baby son

When the shrub roses give away
    their scent generously
      in the evening breeze

While the creaking sound of the crickets is
    reaching us
    in the midst of the night

Let my baby son grow quickly

Let my baby hear the lullaby
    from his mummy

Once the lullaby is finished, my baby

When you become a man

No one will fool you with a lullaby

You'll only fall asleep
    whenever you feel like it

© Firdevs Dede

September 1980 Istanbul

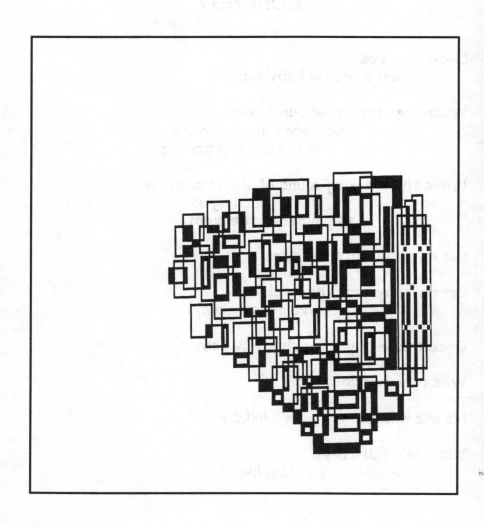

And

Textile Image, Digital Drawing

© Firdevs Dede 2000

AND

And
   she walked towards the infinity
          without any company

Next to the infinity
      no one was left behind
          really

She resembles the sun's uniqueness
      in the universe
         peacefully

© Firdevs Dede

March 1981 Istanbul

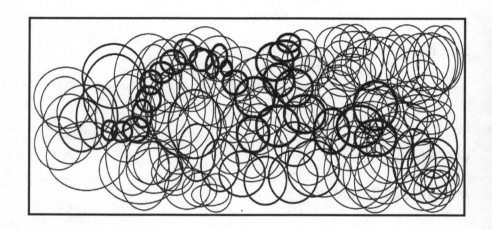

Mistake

Digital Drawing

© Firdevs Dede 2011

A MISTAKE BEYOND REPAIR

If you set out a journey
    for a grandiose fame
        to build up
           for your vanity
              only

Like the women in their heavy make-ups
      sentenced to their false identities
          behind their masks

Once the years pass by
        quickly
          quickly

You'll understand that

It was only a mistake
      beyond a repair
         you made
     at the very beginning
         of your artistic journey

© Firdevs Dede

October 1981 Istanbul

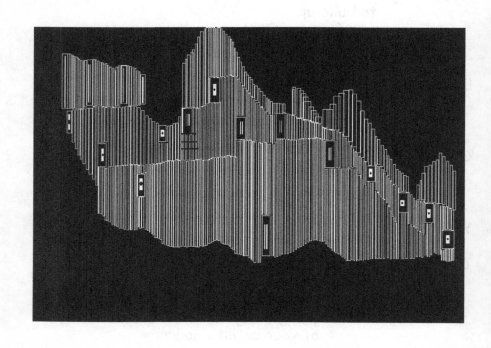

Noise

Digital Drawing

© Firdevs Dede 1998

NOISE

The room is so small
The objects too

The door is opened
The noise is gone

The room is left in tranquillity
    until the noise returns back
        with the creaking sound

© Firdevs Dede

March 1982 Istanbul

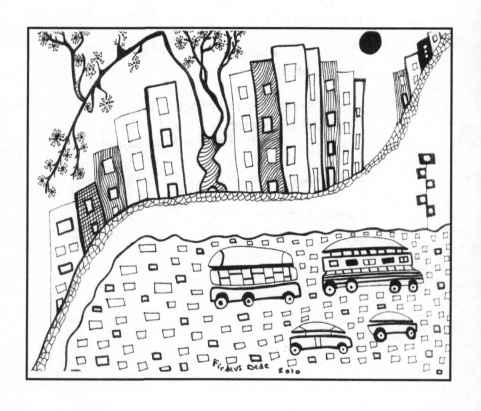

From London

Pen Drawing

© Firdevs Dede 2010

FROM LONDON

—No one can decrease other's loneliness—

Today, I saw the loneliness
            inside a black man's eyes

Yesterday, the loneliness was an Indian girl
                        in her sari

Japanese Miharo hides her loneliness
            within her weak body

When Michael touched his guitar
            at Janet's attic

I heard the scream of the loneliness
                and
        the strong smell of the memories

The long term memories are for a jumble sale now
            in the second-hand dealer's yard

What I saw in the eyes of a black man
            or in an Indian sari
        came with me
            from another country

© Firdevs Dede

December 1984 London

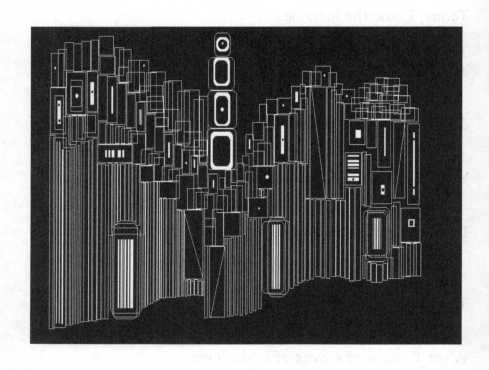

Art is only a DREAM

Digital Drawing

© Firdevs Dede 1998

ART IS ONLY A DREAM

Last night, I had a nightmare
In my dreadful dream
We were all adults
    without knowing how we thought
        or imagined the lovely simple things
           when we were only kids
      like trees
    sky
      moon
        our toys
  or the most colourful places
      like funfairs

Today's duty is to catch up
      with the faded memories
          as much as I can
      of course

It isn't that easy to go back to childhood
          as an adult

Most of the time
    I'm in between

Art is only a daydream for me
      but not more than that!

© Firdevs Dede

1988 London

NEW-BORN HUMAN BEING

Today
    I walked through the cemetery

In there
        I took off my frozen memories
                    my worries
                        and hopes

There is no aching pain of yesterday
                or any expectation for tomorrow

I buried them in one go
Yesterday and tomorrow are dead now
                lying in their graves

Me!
    I'm a new-born human being
                no prejudice
                    no greed
                        no fear
                            no conflict
                    no anger
                no regret

I've only got what I need:
'A pair of fresh eyes for today's life!'

© Firdevs Dede

June 1993 London

Exclamatory Poem

Digital artwork

© Firdevs Dede 2000

EXCLAMATORY POEM

Happiness for me
It's **red** like fire
        sometime
It can be strong **yellow**
        and very bright **blue**
                in the sky

I pick up my favourite colours
        and put them side by side
                on a canvas

I name all my paintings
        with one title
            which is **"happiness"**

I share my delight
        with everybody
            who views the visual outcomes

Sometimes I draw shapes
        with black and white lines

For me happiness can be a triangle
                or a circle
        or a square
        or a rectangle
        or a hexagon
            depending on my mood
                    truly
I love all the geometrical shapes
        with poetical quotations

© Firdevs Dede

1994 London

Answering Odd Questions

Digital artwork

© Firdevs Dede 2000

ANSWERING ODD QUESTIONS

Although my first name is Firdevs
Some people call me "Fi"

When I am asked
    what I do exactly

I often find it hard to explain the things
                                    I do regularly

"I paint and I draw"
    I say with delight

"Is that all?"

"I dream as well"

"Everyone dreams, Fi"

"I dream during the day time"

"You mean daydreams"

"No, I mean real dreams"

"I can't understand you, Fi"

"Some dreams are more real than the concrete reality"

"That is confusing, isn't it?"

"No, it isn't"

"What else do you do, Fi?"

"I observe everything all the time"

"What else?"

"Then I write about what I observe daily"

"Do you do something else?"

"I reflect"

"What about?"

"I reflect on how I perceive the contrasts
                    like life and death
                 sorrow and joy
                    good and bad"

"What else do you do, Fi?"

"I think about finite beings like us
                 on our short visit
          to the infinite nature of time and space"

"You're a bit strange Fi, aren't you?"

"I might be so
     I might be not
          depending on
               how we see things
                    in life
               from our points of view"

"I cannot understand what you're referring to"

"It doesn't matter that much"

"We can always sense the things
        we can't fully understand by logic"

© Firdevs Dede

February 1994 London

Happy Birthday Mum!

Textile Image, Pen Drawing

© Firdevs Dede 2000

HAPPY BIRTHDAY MUM!

To My Mother **HAMDIYE DEDE**

This season is called spring
              down here
Years are defined by dates
              in a rather strange way

What a lovely day to die mum

And what a lovely day to be born in another time

On the 11th May 1997

My beloved mother moved to the time beyond the
present time

Happy Birthday to you mum
    when you are born again
        in the immortals' country
            of the infinity!

© Firdevs Dede

11 May 1997 London

Going Home

Digital Drawing

© Firdevs Dede 1998

GOING HOME

To My Mother **HAMDIYE DEDE**

It's not us
   but our fragile garments
      left behind
        in our tombs

Our spirits are free
   going home
      up to the sky

© Firdevs Dede

May 1998 London

Dedication to my Poet Father

Pen Drawing

© Firdevs Dede 2010

THE POET IS SLEEPING IN KANLICA

To MY Poet Father **DURMUS DEDE**

When the poet was grinding the words
  which were spun with the colourful silk threads
    borrowed from the rainbow
      in his mill

Years were moving swiftly
    in the river of infinity
  like the great noise of the running water
     among the rocks

And the words were being washed in his fountain of love

The poet fell asleep quietly
    without letting anyone know about it

Each morning of a new day in Kanlica
  a nightingale comes near the place
    where the poet sleeps
    and sings a song for him

The poet wakes up
  from his eternal sleep for a while

He becomes a nightingale
    and a tree
   and a sea
  and a poem
    and an unconditional love in Kanlica

While the sun is rising
    while it is raining
        while the wind is blowing
            from one season to another
            from yesterday to the present day

day and night
    night and day
        within the limitation of human life

The poet was here once
He is there now
But he'll be living with us
        in our beautiful memories
                forever

© Firdevs Dede

11 August 1999 London

42

Dedication to my Poet Father

Pen Drawing

© Firdevs Dede 2010

MY POET FATHER

Nothing suited you apart from POETRY
          as you told me once

In your poet dictionary
          the meaning of a winner or a loser
                    is meant different things

In your poetry, you said
          you had never liked money
                    and the grandiose fame

You wanted your eyes to be implanted
                    into the sockets of a young blind
                              for his use
                              once you moved away

You preferred observing this life from a small room
                              with a sooty lamp

In your philosophy you defined
          the difference between being hungry and full
                    was the cost of bread only

You lived like a shepherd from Anatolia
                    with the same intensity of love
                              for the nature
                    in your beloved city Istanbul

My poet father

The first ship which brought you to Istanbul
                    has already completed its journey

That ship is resting at the harbour of eternity
                              like you now

© Firdevs Dede
August 1999 London

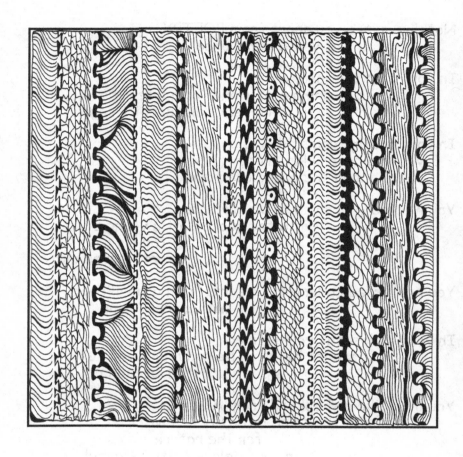

Life is an Incomplete Poem

Each Day

Textile Image, Pen Drawing

© Firdevs Dede 2000

LIFE IS AN INCOMPLETE POEM

EACH DAY

Another beautiful day
            in life

Flowers are singing
Trees are dancing
            outside

Death is in my mind
            but only just

I'm touching
        the sky
            while my both feet
                  staying on the ground

I've completely forgotten
            yesterday

Today is still in my mind

Life is an incomplete poem
            each day

© Firdevs Dede

August 2002 London

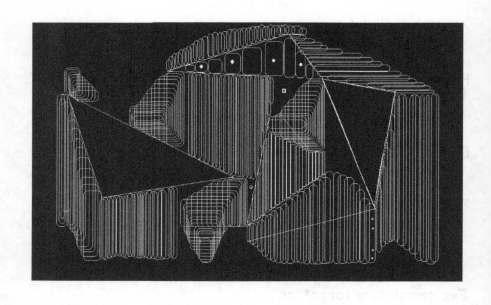

Poem with 365 Lines only

Digital Drawing

THIS IS A POEM WITH 365 WORDS ONLY

This is a poem with 365 words only

It is a year-long poem
               but it didn't take me a year to write

It took me less than 365 minutes actually

What does a word mean?

Does it mean *SOMETHING* or *ANYTHING* at any time?

Today
    tomorrow
           in this century
                  in the next century
                         or
                  at any period
                         of human history

Do we know what the words refer to
               when they are put
                      in a meaningful context?

Getting better in saying something better
                      is a lifelong process
                             to be learnt slowly

Words' constructions in different contexts
                      require perseverance
                             and
                                    a considerable time

Words we know

Words we don't know

Words we understand
       some people might not

Words we like
     some people might not

Words we can hear
      some people might not

Words without any sense

Words with meanings

Words telling us about new concepts

Words resembling the people we know

Words reminding the familiar places

Words appealing to some of us

Words might have lost their meanings

Words need to be reinvented
        within a perspective

Words shouldn't sound bitter

Words should have a healing effect on us

Words should reflect who we are
     and who we are not

Words should signify our deeds

Words should reveal our personalities

Words should say what we can do
     and what we are not able to do

Words should have a vision to hold onto

Words should be used without hostility

Words should be for good days
            and for bad days

Words should be trustworthy

Words should promise the best

Does the silence have a deep meaning for some people?

Silence and words complete one another
            within a meaningful dialogue

Sometimes we mean more
            while we speak less

Sometimes we mean less
            while we talk nonsense

Words can be unnecessary to add

Words can overload our memory

Words can destroy the quiet moment

Words can agitate others

Words can undermine our deeds

Words can alter our peace

Words can cut the silence into the sharp pieces

Words can deteriorate our well beings

Words can breed hostility

Words can make us unhappy

Words can be the most dangerous weapon to be used

© Firdevs Dede

November 2004 London

The Needle Worker's Dictionary

Textile Image, Pen Drawing

© Firdevs Dede 2000

THE NEEDLE WORKER'S DICTIONARY

This is a poem about a dictionary
    the needle worker uses
      while she is creating her needlework
          bit by bit
      day by day
    each year

A is for **Appreciation**
    for the good things we've got in our lives
        like our hopes for the better days
     and our dreams for the days
        we create with our good wills

B is for **Beauty**
    I see in life
      such as
        the beautiful nature of human kinds

C is for **Colour**
    as everything has got the colour of character
          like trees
      plants
     leaves
   and
    the sky

D is for **Decent** things in life
    like trustworthiness
       with transparency
        and
       kindness

E is for **Energy**
> that is necessary
>> for our survival

F is for **Felicity**
> to cherish with

G is for **Generosity**
> when we give our time
>> and
>>> our attention to others

H is for **Honour**
> the decent people earn
>> for their respectable lives

I is for **Ideas**
> we share with one another
>> when we work altogether

J is for **Juxtaposition**
> to juxtapose life and death
>> with contentment and sorrow

K is for **Kindness**
> everyone likes to receive
>> but not easy to return

L is for **Liveliness**
> when we are fit to breathe

M is for **Magnificent**
> for the unusual beauty to be described

N is for **Needle-lace**
> as we all create a needle-lace
>> out of our lives
> with our deeds and words

O is for **Optimist**
> whose nature doesn't allow being otherwise

P is for Peace
    as everyone loves to enjoy it all the time

Q is for Quality
    which is required for the best work

R is for Reliance
    as it's necessary for the peace of mind

S is for Sage
    as we get older
        and wiser
           year by year

T is for Trustworthy
    it's hard to find it amongst unreliable people

U is for Uniqueness
    as everyone and everything is unique by nature

V is for Vision
    for the better things to arrive

W is for Wish
    for a meaningful life with a purpose

X is for Xmas
    to be celebrated in a jolly mood

Y is for Year
    as it is spent consciously
        or unconsciously
           within a calendar time

Z is for Zigzag
    when the life goes up and down
        we experience the zigzag line

© Firdevs Dede

November 2004 London

Nomad Woman

Pen Drawing

© Firdevs Dede 2008

NOMAD WOMAN

The nomad woman was born in Africa

She left there 20 years ago

She is only back to her village for a short visit
   with some presents from America
     where she lives now
    as a well-known celebrity
      for the last 10 years

Look mother
  what I've brought with me
    a beautiful mirror with the silver handle
     just for you to adore your beauty
      that's what women do
     in the civilised country

See mum
  how beautiful
    how adorable you are

You do not want to admire
    your beauty in the mirror!

Why not?

I've brought this mirror for you

I thought you'll be happy
    to see how gorgeous you are!

I've completely forgotten that
   enjoying one's beauty
    is considered VANITY
      in our culture

The nomad women aren't allowed to have such a luxury
                              in their lives

I've changed a lot mother
I thought you've changed too
I thought the whole family has been changed
I thought the whole village has been changed
                        since I was there
                              in America

I can see now mum
        nothing has been changed here
                nothing has been changed for you
                        nothing has been changed
                              in this tiny village

The nomad women have no time
                to cherish their beauties

The nomad women have to work
                day and night

They have no right to make any complaints
                about their lives

The nomad women have to get on with their struggle
                              from one year
                                    to another

Look mother
I've brought you cocoa oil
        to keep your skin soft and fresh,
                isn't that useful for you either?

You prefer the butter from the goat milk
                to put on your face
                        you don't even bother that nowadays

There isn't enough butter to eat
　　　　　　　let alone to put on your face

Sorry mum, how could I know that
　　　　nothing has been changed here
　　　　　　　while I had been changing
　　　　　　　　　　　　over there?

The struggle is the same
　　　　you've been going through in life

Next time mother
　　　　I'll bring more appropriate presents
　　　　　　　for the whole family to enjoy

I'll carry tin food with me
　　　　like tin sardines, tin tuna, tin mackerel,
　　　　　tin pineapples, tin pears, tin plums
　　　　　　　　some potato powder,
　　　　　a few jars of honey
　　　　　　　　and some biscuits for the kids

They'll last long
So every day mum
　　　　there will be something for us all to eat
　　　　　　　at least, when I am on my holiday

You don't need to worry
　　　　how you are going to feed me
　　　　　　　or your whole family
　　　　　　　　without anything at home
　　　　　　　　　　or in the village store

You can keep your precious goats
　　　　without any need to be slaughtered
　　　　　　　for us to eat

59

You'll still enjoy your goats' company
        and get their milk regularly
                to give it to the sick
                        and needy

Goodbye mother
I promise you
I'll be back to visit you all again

Next time I'll come here
        with better presents though

I am a nomad woman
        like you mum
I am connected to you
           and our surroundings
              in the same way
                all the nomad women are

I look at the sky
        and the stars
            with the marvel of my childhood heart

I feel free
    when I live
        on the borrowed time of life
           when I remember your stories
              from my babyhood
        with the healing power of your pure love
           for me and my siblings

Wait for me mum
        don't dare to dye
           till I am back
We'll have a good time
        with full of food in my rucksack
           next time

We'll sit outside in the garden
We'll have barbecue sardines
              on the wood fire
Then we'll have biscuits with honey spread
                    as our dessert afterwards

I'll be back in a year time
Keep well mum!
And be happy as always
Your daughter will remember you
              with the longing
                    for the good old days
                          we had once

A year will pass quickly mother
The summer will come soon
              with sunny days
I'll be at the door with my rucksack
We'll talk about our past
I'll promise you again that
              I'll visit you next summer
                    at the same time

Life goes on and on
        till the last stop
              and we'll all die happily
          without any regret
      for the things we've never tried

© Firdevs Dede

July 2005 London

VOID

There is a void
>   in the brains of patients
>   suffering from the Alzheimer disease

There are missing concepts in their lives

They can't remember how to describe things
>   which used to be done effortlessly
>   before the disease hit them badly

They can't recognise
>   their loved ones

They aren't the same people they used to be

They've become strangers to
>   their previous identities

A daughter or a son of the Alzheimer patients
>   can be very impatient with
>   their parents suffering from the disease

I know it isn't your fault, mum
>   but it isn't my fault either

You aren't the same person I adored as a child

You are different now

You can't even remember me
>   your own daughter
>   or my sister Emily any longer

You confuse me each day
Where is your new dress, mum?
The one I brought you yesterday
Let's put it on you now
I can't stand the state you are in

Hurry up mum, we are going to the zoo this afternoon
You like walking up and down
                    in the zoo

Then we'll go to the toy shop together
I'll be getting you a new toy
Remember you wanted to take Sonia's Barbie doll
                    from her
                        last Sunday
                when she was here with Emily

Mum, please forget what I've said about the fault bit
I still do love you as you are
                just like a little girl
                    when you used to be in your childhood

You're my daughter now
            and my dear mum
                at the same time

I am still your daughter
                as I used to be one
                        even our roles have been changed
                                significantly now

Love is the same
            we both have
                for each other

That hasn't been changed since you've been unwell
Our love has always been unconditional, mum

Tomorrow I'll take you to Emily's place
We'll have tea with Emily and your granddaughter Sonia

On the way,
I'll get a chocolate cake for us all to have with tea
Shall I get a strawberry cake or a lemon cake for you?
Which cake do you fancy, mum?
The trouble is you can't answer me

I often think you understand me
Do you understand what I am talking about?
No or yes?

I don't know what I am talking about either
Doctors said you'll never recover from the loss of memory
How do they know that you won't recover, mum?

Maybe, one day, when I come here to take you around
             you'll call me with my name like you used to
                        before you had lost your memory
                                      completely

You had never called me Nicola
You had always called me Nicky
             as I've been your youngest daughter

You had never called Emma with her proper name either
You had called her Emily since our childhood
You've never got to know Emily's daughter Sonia though
I wonder how you would shorten
                  your granddaughter's name
             Sonny, perhaps

Never mind, mum!
We'll have tea and cake in Emily's home tomorrow
You'll have your own Barbie doll, Sonia will have hers
There won't be anything for you to get upset about
                           while we're out

65

I love you mum as you're
You are my dear mother who requires my attention
                                   all the time

Let's go out now
It'll be good to have a bit of fresh air
                                   for a while

© Firdevs Dede

July 2005 London

Lady Fluffy

Pen Drawing

© Firdevs Dede 2010

LADY FLUFFY

A cat called Fluffy
　　　　was my guest
　　　　　　　for 3 weeks
　　　　　　　　　in August
　　　　　while her owner was away
　　　　　　　during her summer holiday
　　　　　　　　　in the year 2005

I addressed my guest cat as "**Lady Fluffy**"
　　　　　　　　in our cat-like chitchat

She has gone with her owner a minute ago

Tonight, in the absence of my cat friend
　　　　　　I feel like crying

The first night without Fluffy

Without seeing her walking around quietly

Without Fluffy sitting
　　　just opposite me in her armchair
　　　　　　or next to me in the sofa
　　　　　　　which we used to share
　　　　　　　　while she was living with me

I wonder whether Lady Fluffy was a cat
　　　　　　　or a human being
　　　　　　　　but looked like a cat

The cat with the human qualities
　　　isn't different than any human being for me

I collected her fur from the furniture

I saw her broken nails
         and a piece of her moustache
                   left in the carpet

Lady Fluffy doesn't exist in this place
              we both lived together for 3 weeks

The human-like cat has taken away some part of me
                        while she was taken
                                  in her basket

How Lady Fluffy made me feel her presence
                        each time
                   we shared together
              is hard to imagine!

When I came back home from work
                   and
         when I woke up in the early morning
getting ready for work

Lady Fluffy always made me happy

I've just thought about my cat friend's mortality

I feel such a relief that
         Lady Fluffy is still alive
                   but in another place

Knowing the reality doesn't lessen my bereavement
                        for Lady Fluffy
I feel my cat visitor is gone from my life forever

© Firdevs Dede
August 2005 London

Fictitious Character

Pen Drawing

© Firdevs Dede 2008

FICTITIOUS CHARACTERS

Fictitious characters
      in novelists' writings
           might look like real characters
                from life

In ordinary people's lives
      there are a lot of fictitious characters

I wonder how fictitious our lives
           can be in writers' books

It seems to me
      everyone lives their own fantasy
           with its absolute seriousness
                for a while

We only make sense others' invented certainty
           as we go along
              within our realities

Fictions start making sense
      when we meet the fictitious characters
           somewhere in the world
              amongst others

© Firdevs Dede

November 2005 London

RECONCILIATION

All the doors leading us to
                self-destruction
like a grandiose fame and
                lavishing lifestyle
                        are closed for me
                                forever

The only door left wide open
                has no complication

It'll take me safely
                to the Heaven
                        that is my reconciliation

© Firdevs Dede

July 2005 London

Life Cycle Loop by Loop

Textile Image, Pen Drawing

© Firdevs Dede 2000

LIFE CYCLE LOOP BY LOOP

A life cycle knits its realities
                loop by loop

Once we are here
      then we are not
And we'll come back again

A life cycle knits its realities
                loop by loop

A bit of resemblance
A bit of peculiarity
And we'll have a new life soon

A life cycle knits its realities
                loop by loop

A bit of spring
A bit of summer
A bit of autumn
      then it'll be winter again

A life cycle knits its realities
                loop by loop

The time is definite
The time is indefinite
We'll start living our lives
                yet again

© Firdevs Dede

December 2006 London

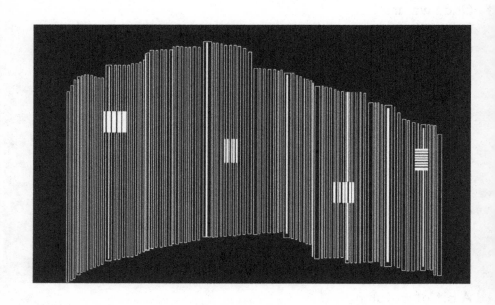

Memoir of Bliss

Digital Drawing

© Firdevs Dede 1998

MEMOIR OF BLISS

Feel the moment of bliss at present
Never mind the gloomy past
Don't bother with the unpredictable tomorrow
Take the day as it comes
Regret not
But live in the moment of bliss as you please

© Firdevs Dede

May 2006 London

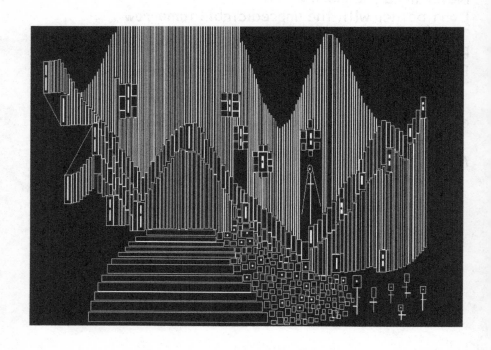

A Long Lasting Research of Life

Digital Drawing

© Firdevs Dede 1998

A LONG LASTING RESEARCH OF LIFE

Do your research on each subject you're most interested
It might be equally viable to do research on the subjects
                              you're least interested
Keep the balance
        between your preferences and your needs
Do your life research constantly
Remember we're all what we know
                  or what we don't know
There is a minor difference between
            what we understand
                  and what we don't understand

Do your research bit by bit
See how much you've learnt each time
    And how much you've already forgotten

© Firdevs Dede

November 2006 London

Learning Resources

Pen Drawing

© Firdevs Dede 2010

LEARNING RESOURCES

My learners and I were the only learning resources
                at some point of my teaching career
                                as a language tutor

I didn't have any equipment
                even a permanent room for my teaching practice
                        or financial resources
                              to buy the essentials

I only lived in my fantasy
                with the possibility of getting
                        some learning resources
                              in the long run

When I entered into the learning environment
                that could be a tiny kitchen
                    or a temporary cold room
                        without any heating on
              forget about the white or black board
                        or the board markers
              or a piece of chalk to be used
                            for writing

Let's start today's session
                with enthusiasm

Forget about the fantastic resources
                      we do not have at present

Instead we can use our imagination
                to replace the board
                      with the unseen equipment
                            in our daydream

We could invent everything
        with the invisible letters of alphabet
                in which we could communicate
                rather well

It didn't matter
    we had no projector
            or PowerPoint slides
                or computers
            in the temporary classroom
        till we were chucked out of the room
    in the midst of the session
        as it happened unexpectedly
                in my teaching career
                        sadly

Do you mind, my dear learners
        if we visit the local library
                this afternoon
            in order to overcome the lack of space
                    we are facing now?

At least we might find a space to continue our session
                    without being interrupted
                            by anybody

I had been a teacher who lived in her fantasy
        by replacing the lack of learning resources
                with the imaginary ones
                        only

I've still got the most beautiful memories
            as a resourceful team member
    without any access to the learning resources
                    for my teaching practice

© Firdevs Dede

February 2007 London

FAILURE

TheMoreYouArePowerfulTheMoreYouArePowerless

HowPowerlessYouAreByFailingOthersWithYourNonsensePolitics

YouAreFailingYourselfEachTimeYouFailOthers . . .

© Firdevs Dede

October 2007 London

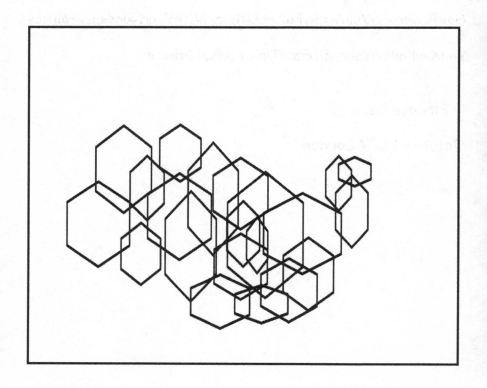

Patching with Happiness

Digital Drawing

© Firdevs Dede 2011

PATCHING WITH HAPPINESS

I had a patching work to do this afternoon

Audrey's present for me from the early nineties

A pair of white cotton trousers
               needed to be patched carefully

The old trousers had wear and tear
               like us
                    I suppose

I had left-over canvas clothes from the old days
            when I used to stretch my own canvasses
                        for painting

The pieces of canvas cloths were turned into the hexagons
                       a few years ago

While I was on a garment making course
              in further education
                  soon after I was made redundant
             from my previous teaching occupation

The three hexagons weren't used for anything
           in those days
               and they stayed in my sewing box
                     for a long while

How strange it was I had the holes in my trousers
           and I had the tree hexagons ready
              to be used for patching my old trousers
        out of necessity
           rather than a deliberate choice

I still felt pleased
    while I was patching
            my old trousers with the holes

Placing the hexagons on the holes carefully
        as though I was painting on canvasses
                years ago

The former one was for the artistic purpose

The latter one was to save the planet

Both purposes suit me perfectly well
        as both occupations filled me
                with satisfaction

I even forgot all my worldly worries
        and sang a song of serenity
                instead

© Firdevs Dede

June 2007 London

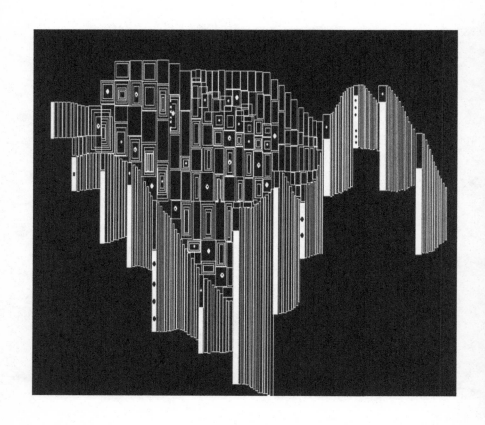

Listen to Your Own Silence

Digital Drawing

© Firdevs Dede 1998

LISTEN TO YOUR OWN SILENCE

It
  is
    so
      nice
        not to have
          a word
            or
              a colour
                or
                  a line
                      for
                     some
                         time

Just listen
     to your own silence
        for a short while

Pause and wait
       for clearing
         your own mind
           till you are ready
              to pour
           some more
              into your container
                 bit by bit

But not all
    at once

Nothing will last longer
      if you overload
          your mind
            UN
                NECES
            SARILY

Unnecessarily!

© Firdevs Dede

June 2007 London

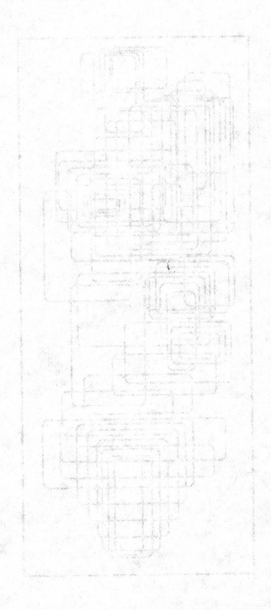

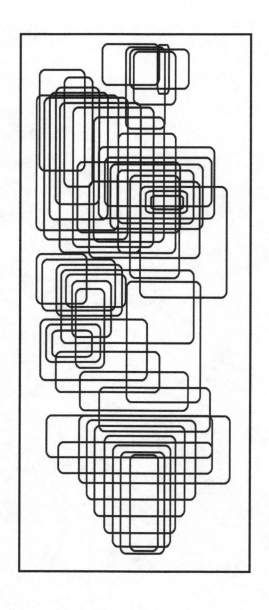

Destiny

Digital Drawing

© Firdevs Dede 2011

DESTINY

Our destiny is not known
        by any of us

We cannot plan our birth
        or the final episode
            of our lives

We all taste the life
      and the death
         which are planned
              beyond our wish
        most of the time

There is nothing
        to be scared of

There is nothing
        to be proud of

We're all vulnerable
        while we face our birth
            or death
        at some points of our lives

There is nothing to be planned
        by us
      for the better
        or the worst
           in life

Everything will happen
        within our destiny
           somehow

© Firdevs Dede

July 2007 London

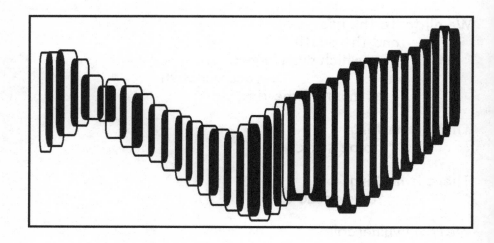

Anima and Animus

Textile Image, Digital Drawing

© Firdevs Dede 2011

ANIMA and ANIMUS

When I see
    the ANIMUS in me
        and other women
            I am very happy

To see the ANIMA in men
        makes me even happier

When a woman becomes
        the total anima
           I cannot stand

If a man becomes the total animus
        I detest the mask of his artificiality

Men and women are only human
        if they are able to touch
    their anima
    and
      animus
        at the same time

© Firdevs Dede

August 2007 London

MY DESERT ISLAND

In the desert island of mine
  I'd like to meet all the wild animals
    in the tamed state of human mind

I'd like them to talk to me
  in 70 human languages
    without thinking
  whether or not
   learning languages
    is
     innate
     or
      social
      or
     environmental act of art

As long as
  they all understand me
    and the other way around
     in the context of animated beings

I don't think I really mind!

Would I ever wish to learn their languages then?

I cannot remember what I thought about that

How am I going ask the lion
  to teach me how to say *HELLO*
    in the lion language?

I might ask my tiger friend
    how to pronounce *MORNING GOOD*
            in the tiger language?

I should request from the whales
        what is the correct way of saying
        HOW DO YOU DO?

If I am going to learn animal languages
            from my animal friends
        what is the point of being
            in a desert island?

The point is
        I'd like my animal friends to speak to me
                    in human languages
                as I'd like to figure out
            how easy
            or
            how difficult
    for the animals to sense
    how it feels to be a human being
when they speak our languages

Will they all forget
        what they mean
            or
        the semantic nature of
                70 human languages?

Never mind the syntactic structure
                for a while

They might even sense
        what they'll be talking about
            better than
    observing each other's behaviours

By the way,
     are we talking about human behaviours
               or
        animal behaviours?

We'd better to identify
     the type of the cognitive process
        we'll be all experiencing
     in the desert island of mine
         where the animal species
    and I will be present
     for finding a common interest to talk about

© Firdevs Dede

August 2007 London

101

ASEPTIC BONE NECROSIS

The price of being a diver in the deep sea
below 100 metres
is your life
my poor lad
with the diagnosis of BONE NECROSIS
which means DEATH BONES in your body
like gangrene

You can no longer move your body

The cost of your life is
so cheap for your employers
while you paid the cost
with an arm and a leg
to dive
below 100 metres

There is no price to pay for your precious life

You're cheaper than the robot divers

Your employers are very clever to cut their cost
by ending your life
which is nothing
in comparison with a robot life

Robots cost more than you and me, perhaps

They get rusty in the deep sea

Your employers can't afford to throw away
a rusty robot

However, they can easily take away
                          your license
                 which is your livelihood
          as they are always inconsiderate

Unfortunately, no-one can stop them
           from exercising their unfairness
                          regularly
                    on their employees

Your employers will be thirsty
           for a new life to be abandoned
                          as useless
     with the cancellation certificate of
     a new diving license
                          which will say that
          'The holder doesn't fit for diving any longer'

By doing so they'll become more thoughtless
                    and more destructive
                          in their actions
The legislation can only support your employers' unfairness

There is no compensation for
                 the loss of your life
                 or
                          your income
                          or
                 your capacity to live
                    or
                 die

You're so cheap
           that was the reason
                 your employer has chosen you
                          instead of a robot
                 to dive below 100 metres

You can congratulate your boss
    on being one of the most corrupted employers
            you've ever worked for

You can write a book of your life-story
            in the deep sea
                and
        how you've lost your ability
                to dive
                    or
                to live
                    purposefully

If your book of life or death
            doesn't sell
Please do not worry!

At least you'll be getting a satisfaction
                by outlining
        how unfair your greedy employers
                have been towards you!

© Firdevs Dede

September 2007 London

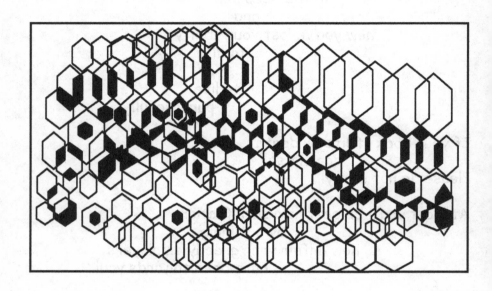

Sleeping Peacefully

Digital Drawing

© Firdevs Dede 2011

I'LL GO TO SLEEP PEACEFULLY TONIGHT

I'll go to sleep peacefully tonight
    without any worry
        for tomorrow
           to catch
              the bus
        or the train
     in the dark
      in the rain
       in the snow
      in the wintertime

I don't care whether it snows
        or rains tomorrow

I had a long day today
I've left my past
      on the shelves though

All the folders for my teaching practice
          are closed down
I'll never touch them again

I'm completely free
      for a new start
         without any worry
    for the weather forecast
  or
the travel news

I'll go to sleep peacefully tonight

I don't care whether it snows
        or rains tomorrow

I've already made my mind

I'll be living for myself
                but not
                        for the useless folders
under any circumstances

© Firdevs Dede

November 2007 London

AUTISTIC CHILD

It's normal to be deaf and blind voluntarily
                    for an autistic child
          within the environment
                    lacking the social stimulation

It's perfectly all right to have an emotional blockage

This isn't your loss
                    but your gain in life

You're stronger than many children
                    who fear being left alone

You know how to be yourself

You can describe the difference
                    in your colourful language
                    better than non-autistic children
You can take a delight in every beginning
                    as it is the end of your routine
You can take a delight in every end
                    as it is the beginning of a new learning

You can sense the things through the joy of discovery

You're only yourself
                    when you are nothing
                    beyond any boundary
                              now and then
Autistic child,
          you'll be overcoming the emotional blockage
                              with a great success
                              eventually

© Firdevs Dede

March 2007 London

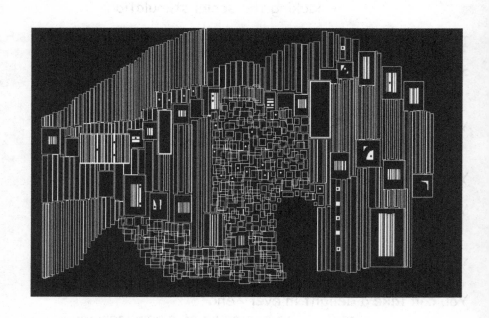

Mourning for the Ancient Tree
without its lovely presence
amongst the concrete buildings

Digital Drawing

© Firdevs Dede 2007

MOURNING FOR THE ANCIENT TREE

I mourned today for the tree I've lost recently
   on the way back home from the university
      when I saw no more
     the tree I had adored
        in the tiny park
      near the bus stop
        in Elephant Castle

The tree was cut off
    so cruelly
      and permanently
I drew the tree from memory
    to lessen my grief
       temporarily

Firdevs Dede

March 2007

MALARIA

Mosquitoes brought the disease
      to the starving babies
            in Kenya, Gambia
   and the rest of the third world countries

The vanishing babies are the symbols
      of the forgotten consciousness
         amongst the modern civilisations

There is no money available for the dying babies
And there is no money for the prevention of malaria
Yet, there is the luxurious *"bed net"*
      which is sold for **$2.00** each
         in the world market

Money needs to be made even out of tragedy
How illogical the civilised conscious is!
When you suffer from malaria and facing starvation
You don't have $2.00 to spare for the *"bed net"*

Did Freud have any analysis of this lack of
   human consciousness
        somewhere in his unpublished notes?

Would have Freud categorised this
    as the *"dysfunctional ego"* of the rich?

Does the refusal of donation for the essentials of
   the needy
     strike any conscious minds in shame?

Where is the *"world fund"* for the "humanitarian *aid?"*

Will the rich and the fit wait for the whole world
      to be completely destroyed
       before it'll be too late to save the needy
   from their sufferings such as malaria,
lack of nutrition, lack of sanitary

lack of medical facilities, lack of water
lack of education, lack of human dignity
in the forgotten global villages of the faraway countries

In Kenya, for example
The patients need to bring their own water
on admission to hospital
for treatment
which doesn't exist
in any case

The medical team members are asked to
perform the miracles
in the absence of the medical facilities

Hospital beds are full of dying patients
yet, the cure such as malaria is so simple

Do we really need to wait for the world epidemic?
Waiting patiently without being questioned
by our super ego
is the only answer we can come up with
for today's urgent problems
on a global scale

That must be the sign of our desensitised
or unresponsive human emotions
to the economic crisis

We can only blame the modernity for it
which has turned most of us
into insensitive subjects
with dysfunctional senses
It is not possible to feel the pain any longer
in hearing of the unresolved conflicts
for human sufferings

We all suffer from alienation of others' needs
We've completely forgotten to raise
not only *"self awareness"*
but *"awareness of others' sufferings"*

We are lost without our emotions
        for positive responses
            to each other's needs

The final dilemma
        of our human mind
                ignores malaria
            and other curable diseases
        in the faraway countries
            of our old world
            without taking any responsibility
    whatsoever!

© Firdevs Dede

June 2007 London

115

PROFESSIONAL DEVELOPMENT JOURNAL

I recorded in my "Professional Development Journal"
Nothing is impossible for a facilitator
    working with the learners who have got
            specific learning difficulties
Anyone can learn anything at any time
            to acquire life skills for survival

The left hemisphere of brain
And the right hemisphere of brain
            work equally well
        in accordance with
    the learners' learning preferences

Both hemispheres of our brains perform brilliant jobs
            depending upon their functions
through multi-sensory learning materials
        on the lifelong learning programme

© Firdevs Dede

February 2007 London

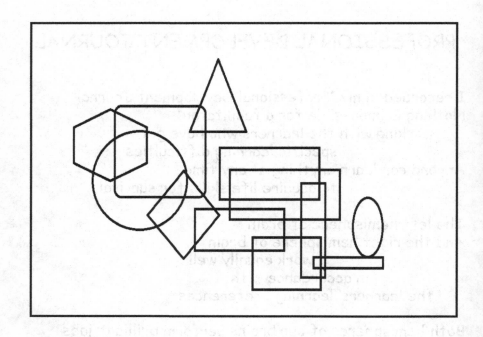

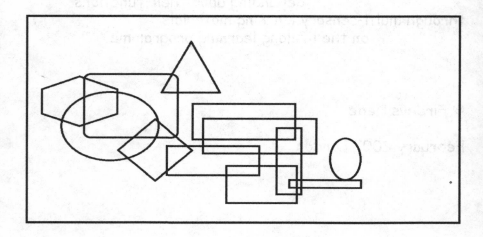

Day Out

Digital Drawing

© Firdevs Dede 2011

DAY OUT

I was waiting for the bus
    in Bermondsey bus-stop at 1.30 p.m.
        to take me all the way to Holborn
            on the 28th Oct 2008

I spent more than 45 minutes
    seeing the 5 buses going to the wrong direction
        and none was available to take me
            to the British Museum

I got irritated a bit
    with a good reason

While the passengers ran out of patience
    a nice lad passing by
        warned us

"By the way you'll be waiting for ages
    there is congestion
        near the tube station"

I decided to walk up to Bermondsey station unwillingly

It was already 2.30 p.m.
    when I reached the station hastily

I was at the British Museum by 3.00 p.m.
    exactly

There was still two and a half hours left
    to the museum's closing time
        at 5.30 p.m.

I took the lift to the room 90
    to see the Western prints and drawings
        from the museum collection

I didn't know
            the museum has 3 million items

            dating from about 1400
                        to the present day

I admired the work from Ben Nicholson
            called *'A Plate of Pears'*
            done in 1955
            oil paint over pencil
            and his dry point entitled
"San Gimignano" done in 1951'

There was a good gouache & watercolour from
                        John Hoyland
            named *"Abstract Composition on a Red Background"*
                        done in 1966

I loved Barry Flangan's etching done in 1983
                        entitled *"Mule"*
            and his lithograph produced in 1970 called
"Orange Dusk"

What a nice surprise for me to glance at
                        Ian Hamilton Finlay's
                        "Star/Steer"
            the first time in my life
                        even it was done in 1966

What a good poet Ian Hamilton must have been
            while he was producing the poster prints
                        using his own poetical text
                        which are 19
                        in the British Museum

Finlay had a great influence on
            the concrete poetry movement
                        says the introductory note
            beneath his work

How good it was to see the wife and the husband
        juxtaposed with their distinctive drawings

    which are totally different
        from one another

Husband Kenneth Martin produced
      his serial drawings
        all abstract
      with ink and brush
        in 1958

Artist's wife Mary Martin produced
        "Permutation"
          in 1965
using the basic element of the triangle
     to create an abstract formation
       in ink over graphite
       with white gouache

The wife's work is a bit complicated
     in the most beautiful way

The husband's work is a bit simplistic
     in the most beautiful way

Nevertheless they both achieved to say
       what they wanted to say
        in the most original way
Lines are different
Lines are beautiful
Lines are unspeakable
Lines are colourful
Lines are monochromatic
Lines are expressive
Lines are grand

On the way back home with the delight of happiness
      from my short trip
        to the British museum

All the images left their traces in my visual memory

I went to bed as early as 8.00 o'clock
in the evening
to see the drawings all over again
in my dream

I woke up at 1.00 a.m. to write this poem
called "**Day Out**"

When I read the poem from time to time
I'll be remembering the unforgettable day of mine
at the British museum
which represents
all the ancient civilisations
and the pre-historic periods of the human race

The rooms in the British Museum take us
from one period to another
with all the artefacts
as the proofs of our ancestors' history
speaking their own tongues
making their own gestures in order to say that

"**We all lived once**"

from one period to another . . .

and

"**We are still around amongst you all now!**"

© Firdevs Dede

October 2008 London

DREAMS without Censorship

Textile Image, Pen Drawing

© Firdevs Dede 2000

DREAMS WITHOUT CENSORSHIP

When I paint a picture
　　　or draw a line
　　　　　and write a poem
I am as free as I should be

There is no censorship in my dreams
I could be a child
I could be an adult
I could be young
I could be old
I could be a flower
I could be a leaf
I could be the sun
I could be the moon
I could be a fish
I could be a bird
I could be me
I could be someone else
I could be here and now
I could be there and then
I could be nothing
I could be everything
I could be a joy
I could be a pain

As I said earlier
　　　there is no censorship in my dreams
　　　　　when I paint a picture
　　　　or draw a line
　　　　　and write a poem such as this one
I could be everywhere
I could be up in the heaven
I could be down on this earth
I could fly like an albatross
I could swim like a dolphin

I could cry without any inhibition
I could laugh wholeheartedly
I could live forever
I could die whenever I want to
I could sing a song
I could recite a poem
I could do everything
There is no censorship in my dreams

© Firdevs Dede

October 2008 London

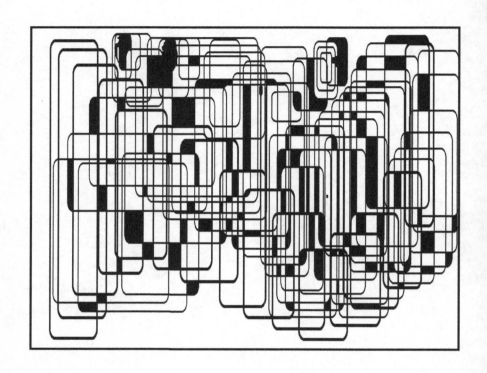

Imagination

Digital Drawing

© Firdevs Dede 2011

IMAGINATION

I imagine a country in which
    everyone's uniqueness is accepted
        wholeheartedly
I imagine a country in which
    no one treats anyone
        unjustly

I imagine a country in which
    the freedom of choice can't be restricted

I imagine a country in which
    everyone lives happily

I imagine a country in which
    everyone can trust anybody

I imagine a country in which
    everyone's contribution
        gets rewarded fairly

I imagine a country
    everyone travels safely

I imagine a country which is
    very close to my vision
        for a better life
    for the whole humanity
        men and women
    the poor and the rich
  the old and the young
    united without any hostility

© Firdevs Dede

July 2008 London

EXCEPTIONAL CASE

Generally speaking
There are two types of people
                    in life
The bullies and the bullied ones

If we do not wish to be
            neither a bully nor a bullied one

We need to avoid the pitfalls of
                any stereotyped existence
        that is an exceptional case
                most of the time

© Firdevs Dede

July 2005 London

TURTLE AND BROOM

I saw a toy turtle
    on top of the wooden wine container
I saw the large broom
    which was placed next to the toy turtle

I've got the analogy all right
    the broom represents my art
      the turtle represents me
        as an artist
      with the slow movements

I prefer moving progressively
      with slow motions
        without running out of steam
          in a very short time

© Firdevs Dede

June 2008 London

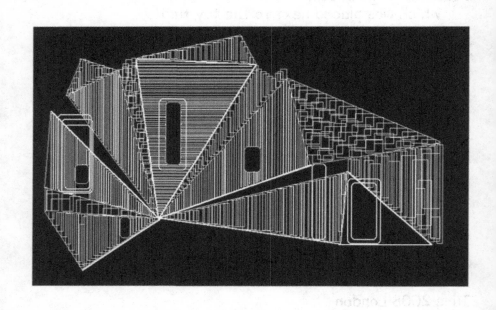

The Melting Pot of This Century

Digital Drawing

© Firdevs Dede 1998

THE MELTING POT OF THIS CENTURY

We're all in the melting pot of this century
                men and women
        critics
     writers
  poets
    and painters

The world is boiling now
      with uncertainty
         more than ever

It's getting harder to find our feet
        on the smooth ground

© Firdevs Dede

June 2008 London

DOUBT

Someone asked an old friend
 "Would you like a cup of life or a cup death to drink?"

Her answer was that
    "She had enough of everything
        offered to her in resentment"

What is the cost of mockery?

Can anybody explain it to her clearly now?

I doubt it!

© Firdevs Dede

June 2009 London

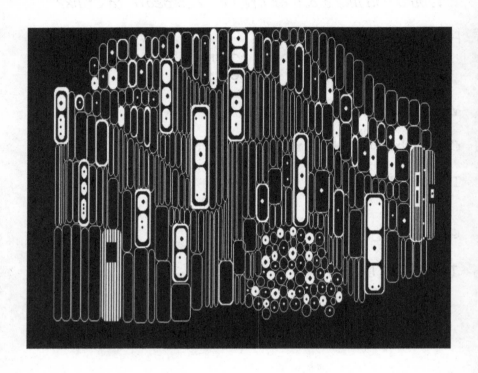

Autumn Leaves

Digital Drawing

© Firdevs Dede 1998

AUTUMN LEAVES

Years ago
    I collected the autumn leaves

They were placed in my sketchbook
        to be viewed occasionally

Years later
    when I look at them
        their beautiful shapes
           give me a pleasure

Yesterday
    when I went for a walk
           in the park
I took a delight in seeing autumn leaves, plants
           and the bees there
I only picked up the dead leaves
        to keep reminding me
           their fragile beauty

© Firdevs Dede

September 2009 London

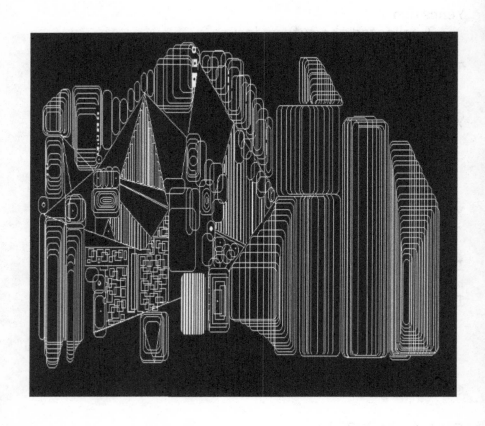

Mathematical Problem

Digital Drawing

© Firdevs Dede 1998

MATHEMATICAL PROBLEM

Life is like a mathematical problem to be solved
                              every single day

Neither you nor I can interfere with each other's life
                              in any way

I
    You
        They
            We
                All of us
            need to solve the mathematical problems
                    we all face in our lives

Time flies

We have no time for a destructive war

We have no time for hatred for one another

We've only got one world to live after all

There is no any other planet to go to

Let's restore the world peace all together
                without postponing today's duty
                              for tomorrow

© Firdevs Dede

December 2009 London

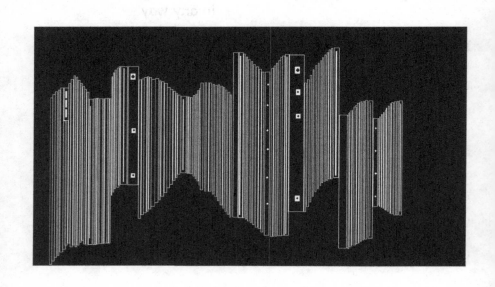

Limited Time

Digital Drawing

© Firdevs Dede 1998

LIMITED TIME

We've got only 365 days within a year

We've got 3,650 days within a decade

If we're lucky enough to live a century
within our lifespan

Then we've got 36,500 days only
that is not a lot!

Years don't last long

Be time-conscious
and avoid wasting the limited time
like water

No matter how hard we stretch the days,
months and years
we only got 365 days a year

With a good timing
I might get some more work done
before I say goodbye to this life

© Firdevs Dede

March 2010 London

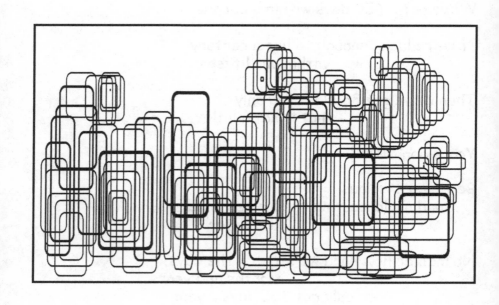

Breakthrough

Digital Drawing

© Firdevs Dede

April 2011

BREAKTHROUGH

I've got more to say
    more to write
       more to describe
         more to sing
           more to laugh
    that's a breakthrough
but not a breakdown!

© Firdevs Dede

January 2010 London

DIET

My diet differs from others
    apricot and watermelon
        figs and grapes
            my summer fruits
            for example

Tomatoes and cucumber
      with spring onions
    all go very well with lemon juice
           and extra-virgin olive oil
        during the summer time

Dried black-eye beans
        and lentils in salads
    a few days a week in winter
          with pasta and rice

Fresh mint, thyme and parsley
    how refreshing they all are
        within the natural yogurt
            cucumber and garlic
        during the spring time

The dishes with green beans
    leeks, courgettes and fresh peas
          will go rather well
        alongside the crushed wheat

Raisins, almonds and sesame seeds
        all give energy to my weak body

An apple
    a pear and a few prunes
        make life easier for me

before and after each meal
throughout the seasons

It's the yolk of the soft-boiled eggs
gives the real taste
when I have it
each morning
with the half of a bread slice

The other half of it is left for me
to have it with honey
with a cup of sage tea

I eliminate the red meat
and the chicken
from my daily food intake

Sardines and mackerels
every other day
with salad and rice

How can I overlook the dried onions
with pack of antioxidants?

That is my diet
which only makes sense
when I've got enough money left
in my pocket
after paying the bills and the rent

© Firdevs Dede

September 2010 London

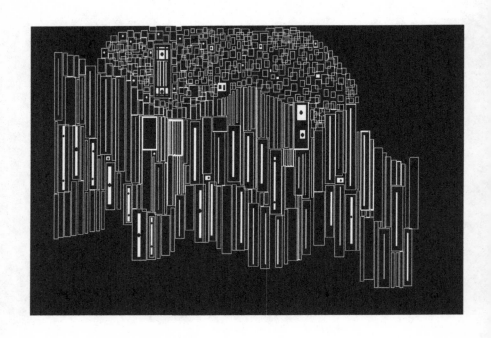

Waiting Eagerly

Digital Drawing

© Firdevs Dede 1998

WAITING EAGERLY

It's mid-autumn now
It's raining again
The winter hasn't arrived yet
I am not complaining
I'll be waiting eagerly
    for the next summer to arrive

It'll only take
    9 months
        for the good weather
            to return us
      and for only 3 months
            to stay with us

© Firdevs Dede

October 2010 London

Barbara Hepworth Sculpture Garden in St Ives

Photographic artwork

© Firdevs Dede 2010

THE UNFINISHED JOURNEY

My journey started from St Ives last autumn
I walked in the harbour
I watched the seagulls waiting for their meals
                    left over fish and chips
                from the tourists
                    visiting Cornwall
                in the late afternoon

I watched the young lovers exposing themselves to
                    the warmth of the sun
            by the sea

I watched the sailing boats on the sand
            looked like someone carried them all
                        by hand

I discovered how the sculptor Hepworth
            carved her stones in Trewyn Studio in St Ives
        with the greatest affection for her material

Hepworth museum was a home for both artists
                and their triple children
            at the outbreak of the Second World War
                    in 1939

How sad I was not to find any work from Ben Nicholson
                at Barbara Hepworth Museum!

I found more information about Nicholson
                    at St Ives's local library
                on the way back to the holiday village
            where I stayed in a small chalet

My lunch was the Cornish pastry with vegetable fillings

I had a Cornish ice-cream
                with the vanilla zest
                        made from Jersey milk
                                as my dessert

The mint tea with a scone in a cafe
                overlooking the Portmeor Beach
                                by the Tate Gallery
                freshen my journey rather well

I couldn't visit the Tate as it was closed
                                for the refurbishment

It'll be a good excuse for me
                        to go back to St Ives
                                just to see the Tate
                when it is open for public

I had another good day at Carbis Bay
                                the next day

I walked by the sandy beach
                feeding the seagulls with the bread crumbs
                                watching their enjoyment
                provided a memorable treasure for me to remember

I said to myself
                I'd definitely come back here
                                one day

I was in Isle of Wight on the 5th Oct 2010

I immortalised Ventnor and Shanklin
                by capturing their beauty
                                with my digital camera

I had tea in the Heritage Garden
                where Jane Austen had her tea
                                centuries ago

I walked down the Steephill road in Ventnor
where Charles Dickens
spent his summer vacation

I wished to go back there again
to explore the romantic place
near the botanic garden
with Charles Dickens's eyes

I spent 4 days in Ilfracombe
from the 11th Oct 2010
to the 14th Oct 2010

I loved the rocks of the sea
and the farmhouse kitchen restaurant
where I had the homemade soup
with the delicious crispy bread in North Devon

I stayed at the Victorian Lane Hotel
in Brighton
on the 6th Nov 2010
having my breakfast
overlooking the English Channel

It was a joy to visit the Brighton Art Gallery
and sharing my lunch
with the seagulls
by the Brighton Pier

I made my mind that
I would go back
to the same hotel in Brighton
on my birthday

Due to the last minute change
I flew to Guernsey on the 21th Feb 2011
to remark the anniversary of my 52

In Guernsey, it was such a fun to discover
              Victorian Library Priaulx
                 which was converted from
              the Georgian Townhouse
                 in 1889

The historic library building looked grand
                 with its beautiful fireplace
                    and ancient books

I spent a good few hours there
              without getting bored

The unfinished journey of my life
              will carry on
         till the end

A new journey to the new places
              will enrich my life
              with the splendid memories

For an artist
   each journey is an inspiration
                 for her artwork
              to be produced lovingly

Each place adds its colour
                 to the artist's palette
                    to be used later on
              in a painting
                 or a poem
              or a novel

Each journey is worthwhile
         in the diary of an artist

An artist won't get tired of
        the unfinished journey
            of the self-discovery

An artist will be living
        happily ever after
            in her unfinished journey

© Firdevs Dede

April 2011 London

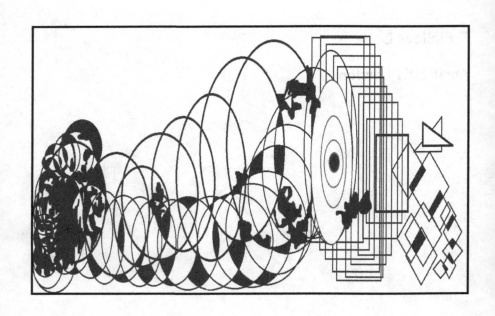

Time Upon Time

Digital Drawing

© Firdevs Dede 2011

TIME UPON TIME

Living the late summer of my maturity
in the same way I had
earlier on
at the beginning of my life

Without any fear of discovery
what life is
or the purpose of being here and now

One's life cycle goes on and on
while we develop
while we learn
while we make sense of our lives
we are the same person
from yesterday
or
we are the ones
who move from
one place to another
and
only recognise ourselves
when we look at our past

© Firdevs Dede

March 2008

THREE CLOCKS AT HOME

Tic-Tac
    Tic-Tac
        Tic-Tac
The clock in the living room
              reminds me
        how long it takes
           to enjoy a good movie
                on the telly

Tic-Tac
    Tic-Tac
        Tic-Tac
The clock in the kitchen
          tells me
           how long it takes
      to enjoy a delicious meal

Tic-Tac
    Tic-Tac
        Tic-Tac
The clock in the bedroom
    enables me to start a new day
              precisely

Tic-Tac
    Tic-Tac
        Tic-Tac
Each clock has got a heart
      I hear the heart beatings
           day and night
        all the time

Tic-Tac
    Tic-Tac
       Tic -Tac
My internal clock
      and
the clocks on the walls
       are in tune
         thankfully
           gleefully

© Firdevs Dede

January 2011 London

ASSERTIVENESS

On the day I visited the Dulwich Art Gallery
I popped into a tearoom for a quick tea
                    and a tiny scone
to build up my energy

It was good to have something in my tummy
It was too much to be asked
        to pay five pounds and fifty penny
                        exactly

I asked the young lady
                    to itemise the bill for me
Her boss appeared with the calculator and the menu
I was pointed at the prices
                quite rightly

It was understood that I was overcharged
The matter was settled quietly
            without any fuss from both sides
Neither part felt angry
            for the mistake made hastily

I was happy to receive two pounds and fifty penny
        which was less than five pounds and fifty penny
                    I was asked to pay originally

I stopped in Lewisham to get small items
        for my daily usage
Assertiveness paid a dividend
I enjoyed my day tremendously
        with an adequate spending power
                for my tea
                    and shopping around
        without being short of money

© Firdevs Dede
May 2011 London

The Queen of the World Literature

Digital Drawing

© Firdevs Dede 2000

THE QUEEN of THE WORLD LITERATURE

The queen of the word literature felt
      as though she had lived a century or two

The ancient poet hasn't worn out yet
She has left the longest leap to her last day

There might be revitalization
       while breathing poetry
         with the fine breeze
    coming from the seaside
      in each settlement she visits

The native seagulls fly willingly
      over the poet's head
   as picking up bread crumbs
      from her hands
    screaming joyfully
in the far distance of her dreams

© Firdevs Dede

May 2011 London

DAILY PRAYER

There is no zigzag line in my life
There is only one single straight line
I've put all my confidence in **You** alone
        and my faith in **Your Glory**
    as You've always answered my prayers
        generously!

Let me glorify **Your Name**
    now and forever

There is only one single line which will take me
        where **You** are
I'll be up there eventually
    without giving up
      my confidence in **You**

There is no zigzag line
    to consume me
      in a destructive falsehood
There is no any other line
    except one straight line
      which will lead me up there
        where **You** are

There is only one **Divine Truth**
    that is my love for **You** alone
My precious **Heavenly Father**
Let me live for **Your Glory**
    in every aspect of my life
      now and forever
       Amen!

© Firdevs Dede

March 2011 London

Death has no power upon me

Digital Drawing

© Firdevs Dede 1998

DEATH HAS NO POWER UPON ME

How comforting it is to know that
           death has no power upon me

I am not obsessed with any materialistic possessions
I have no fear of dying in any way either

I am completely free from
           all forms of destructions

Whenever my journey
           comes to the end

I'll be the happiest person
           leaving a fulfilled life behind
        by overcoming the limitations of my mortality

© Firdevs Dede

July 2005 London